I0478531

Secret Email Marketing.

Practical Methods For Increasing Subscribers.

Effective Steps - Increased their Email Subscribers!

Expert Email-Marketing
Oleg Kolpakov.

Seo: Email Marketing

By Oleg Kolpakov

Published by Oleg Kolpakov at Createspace

Copyright © 2016 by Oleg Kolpakov

Table of Content:

Step 7. Audio-marketing:

Step 8. Buttons of social networks:

Step 9. The script "Tell a Friend:

Step 10. Video marketing:

Step 11. Free e-books:

Step 12. Article marketing:

Step 13. More, Render:

Step 14. Write interesting and often:

Step 15. Mailing Services:

Step 16. Properly position yourself:

Step 17. Forums:

Step 18. Interviews with experts:

Step 19. Ask your subscribers:

Step 20. Own Affiliate Program:

Conclusion:

Introduction:

You took the time to download this book and learn the material.

This means that you are no longer a random passer-by!

This guide will help you to increase the number of subscribers to your newsletter.

The main thing you are required to care and the ability to immediately implement the knowledge gained!

Read and study this book will take you some time, and in the future to save months of work.

The book described 20 effective and identities of steps that will lead you to the result of the construction of the signature base 10000+ email subscribers!

Expert Email-Marketing
Oleg Kolpakov.

All material is unique and has helped many businessmen info.

So get started!

Hello!
Thank you for purchasing my book.

I promise you that you will learn many new and interesting things in this direction.

Expert Email-Marketing
Oleg Kolpakov.

Step 1. Create a capture page:

One of the most effective models of the transformation of the visitor of your site to the subscriber is the system of "capture pages".

What's the point?

You create a separate one-page mini-site is to make the visitor subscriber.

Such a site should not be external links

Internal links.

At the visitor of this site should be only two choices:

1) Become a subscriber.

2) Go to the site.

Let the first person secure for you and become subscribers, but after it with you and discover the very newsletter.

The most interesting. That this working model,

This allows to significantly increasing the number of subscribing your mailing.

What should be on the capture page?

1. Cling to the title;

2. The subtitle;

3. Visual effect (photo, video, 3D cover).

This is a very important part of the capture page.

Everyone likes everything beautiful and desirable volume.

4. Attractive subscription form.

Never insert template boring, terrible subscription form. It is better to pay the designer.

5. Guarantee anti-spam.

So explain to the person and give the assurance that their data will not be used for spam.

6. The lack of external and internal links.

7. List of benefits.

Why subscribe?

What will?

What are the benefits?

What are the benefits?

Literally, 3-5 points are enough.

Step 2. Enter Personal Website (Blog):

On your blog, you can solve a number of important tasks:

1) Proper positioning;

2) Attracting Subscribers;

3) Communicate with auditorium

4) Create a constant influx of new subscribers.

If you write useful materials on a regular basis and optimize the articles for keywords, then after a few months you will provide yourself the constant influx of new subscribers through targeted search engine.

 A blog can be created as a charge or free of charge.

Important recommendations for blogging: - write on a regular basis;

- Write interesting;

- Encourage people to leave comments;

- Organize competitions;

- Use a variety of formats (text, audio, and video);

- Write unique content;

- Establish a collection of subscribers from.

Expert Email-Marketing
Oleg Kolpakov.

If you do all of this will follow in a couple of months, the influx of new subscribers to your newsletter is guaranteed.

Step 3. The form of subscription on every page:

When someone lands on your site, it should be possible to subscribe absolutely site.

Why does it?

The task of your website, your blog in the first place to turn visitors into subscribers.

Expert Email-Marketing
Oleg Kolpakov.

Therefore, make emphasis on the fact

That opportunity was to sign on each page,

And the very form of subscriptions stood out against the background of all the other materials from the site.

Step 4. Offer a mini-book in exchange for a subscription:

The days when people subscribe to a weekly or monthly newsletter passed.

Now everyone wants to get everything at once, and more!

So give them what they want!

One of the options is a bonus mini-book.

Get instantly book much more interesting than just subscribe to some newsletter. People like getting something right.

The book should not be any huge, enough 10-20 page text.

If you are good at your subject, then write such a volume of information you will not be difficult.

Maximum 1-3 hours of your time.

The presence of the book greatly increases your credibility.

The presence of the book increases your expert in the eyes of others.

It would even create a 3D cover for your mini-book. Then the number of those wishing to enter your information will rise sharply.

Step 5. Commentaries on another blog:

Find online top 5 blogs in your niche with the attendance of at least 100-200 people a day.

After that, every day, leave at least 5 comments on this blog each. The result is about 25 comments per day.

It did not take long, but it can bring a good result.

Expert Email-Marketing
Oleg Kolpakov.

When you leave a comment, you can specify the address of the site.

But not in the comments and in your name.

That is, if someone is interested in your comment, decided to find out who wrote it, he clicks on your name and gets on your specified site.

 I recommend specifying a link to your blog.

In order to maximize light up on other people's blogs,

Arrange various discussions, ask questions,

Reply to the comments of others.

In other words, how to be more noticeable.

Write really sensible comments rather than just "Yes, cool art". Often, these comments were not moderated.

Good work comments that are contrary to the general opinion of other blog readers.

Write comments on a regular basis, only, in this case, you will get a good result.

Step 6. Popup-window:

Popup window or a pop-up window - a great way to increase conversion visitor / subscriber at all your sites.

Someone refers to the method, well; someone denies it, explaining that it is very annoying.

To be honest, the figures show only that this technique can increase the number of new subscribers at the same rate of traffic by 1.5-2 times.

How do you like it?

If you have not already, begin immediately. Otherwise, you just lose subscribers and as we have seen,

*Expert Email-Marketing
Oleg Kolpakov.*

Subscribers = money.

On the technical side to implement, it also not makes you easy.

Now there are a lot of different scripts of pop-ups.

Script: Popup-domination (popupdomination.com).

This is a paid script.

But if you do not want to pay, you can use free devices.

Step 7. Audio-marketing:

Very interesting way to attract subscribers and there you will hear a few places.

Step 1.

Get audio tape on services.

Step 2.

Every day, write down a useful audio podcast.

Step 3.

Correctly fill in a description of each podcast.

Include the description of the Audio + link to your capture page.

These audio services are quite untwisted projects with a good daily attendance.

If you publish any audio, this is indicated in the Newswire service.

So you can get a large number of plays your audio for free.

Naturally, most of these students become interested in your content and move to your site, which already subscribes to our newsletter.

Plus a large number of audio materials may affect the attitude towards you as an expert in a particular subject.

Step 8 buttons of social networks:

Expert Email-Marketing
Oleg Kolpakov.

Every year, the effect of the promotion of the social networks is becoming more and more.

This is explained by the fact that almost everyone has free access to the internet; there are pages in several networks, which are checked several times each day.

This must be used for their own purposes.

This can be done through social networking buttons

Correctly placing them on their websites.

There are several varieties of social buttons. As a rule, they are divided on the "Share" and "Like".

What's the Difference? A share button allows you to send a link and write a comment on his hand on the wall in the social network.

The button "Like" automatically publishes on your wall link to the site that you choose to share.

Because social networking is advisable to use Facebook and Twitter.

These social networks are currently dominant on the Russian Internet.

Each of these social services. Networks represent a huge community of millions of people.

Even if your stuff is really helpful and pleasant to all, it does not mean that everything will click on the social networking buttons.

You need to give a clear command to click "here" and "here's here."

Expert Email-Marketing
Oleg Kolpakov.

If you're constantly reminded that you need to talk about your material to all your friends on social networks, then your readers will do it.

More desirable steps to tell you how to do it.

I would also like to draw your attention to the fact, which has social networking buttons.

Make it so that they stand out and are just after your useful material.

If this article, after article put buttons, and in the article itself, remind them.

If this video, immediately below the video button place for all videos on your site visitor will see more and click "Like".

Firstly, it once will want to click on this beautiful button, and secondly, there is

Expert Email-Marketing
Oleg Kolpakov.

some effect of suggestion. Even if the key people and clicks, but the video it probably like it :) And it is also.

Alternatively, you can reward those who share with their friends on social networks your materials.

To do this, prepare some attractive bonus on your topic.

It can be a book, a video, audio, consultation, software, etc.

Step 9. The script "Tell a Friend":

The script "Tell a Friend" is one of the ways to create viral traffic to your site.

The basic meaning is the need to send 3-5 invitations (invitations can set any) in order to get some useful material for free.

There are two options: The first option you give a free bonus in return for a few emails- recommendations to friends.

In the second case, you give a free bonus if 3 people will go to the link in the letters. That is, in this case, the important thing is not the number of sent invitations,

Namely the quality of the recommendations.

Expert Email-Marketing
Oleg Kolpakov.

I'm more inclined to the second option, as often many (me too) has some personal email address. And if to get the bonus, simply send a 3-5 email invitation; it is likely that the majority of them will be sent to your mailbox.

IMPORTANT: To at least someone started to send an email, the recommendations

   The bonus must be really high-quality and useful.

If you are giving a bonus book, which can be downloaded on the Internet at every turn, this is hardly anyone that will stimulate action.

Step 10. Video marketing:

One option to quickly make them known and to collect a large subscriber base is video marketing.

Record now video can absolutely everyone.

This can be withing an ordinary camera, web camera, or record what you have going on right now on the screen.

Also, you can record and upload to the Internet, records of seminars, workshops, master classes, which you spend.

In each video, you can specify a description and links to your sites, where people will have to subscribe to the mailing list.

This method is remarkable in that it is absolutely free.

But in order to quickly get traffic using video, you need to be able to create "viral" video,

Information about which spreads by word of mouth.

To see what the difference between these rollers,

Go to YouTube and analyze videos with multi-million dollar view.

Begin to drive your channel and regularly laid out new videos.

Expert Email-Marketing
Oleg Kolpakov.

Make it so that you were on the internet at every step.

And then the chances are that you will learn about and subscribe to your newsletter, increase significantly!

Step 11. Free e-books:

Plan of action:

1) Write a mini-book program in WORD or any other text editor.

10-20 pages are enough;

2) To check the text for errors;

3) Insert description of the projects and references to "capture page";

4) Compile a book in PDF-file (using the PDF Creator program.

5) To make the announcement of the book on the basis of the existing subscribers;

6) To make the announcement in all the social networks;

7) To make the announcement on the discussion forums;

8) Repeat all steps.

After some time of your book will tell

Spread on blogs, forums, on the torrent, sites, etc.

The more books you run the Internet, the greater will be the result.

Although there is a number is not a determining factor.

Some unique information or the same information,

Which is contrary to public opinion, will diverge on the internet very quickly.

Step 12. Article marketing:

If you can write an article (if not, immediately start to train and practice), you can text your creations effectively used for promotion on the Internet.

At the end of each article, you can insert a description of your projects

Expert Email-Marketing
Oleg Kolpakov.

with links to sites where you have the opportunity to subscribe to the mailing list.

Submit an article on the forums can be on his blog and article directories.

If you type in Google "catalog items", then you will give thousands of sites where you can post articles absolutely free.

If you have an assistant, then you can add articles delegate.

In addition to article directories, articles can be placed on the social networks in the notes.

I recommend placing only the announcement of the article (2-3 paragraphs) with a link to the full version. As you know, the full version will be on your blog, which is a form of subscription and a pop-up window.

After creating a series of articles, you can compile them from the e-book to make it 3Doblozhku and run on the Internet.

Also, each article can tell a voice and put it on an audio blog, we talked about earlier.

And what if you create under each article a few slides and record a screencast? Here you have more content in the same format. And as you already know, the video is very well can be used for promotion and attracting visitors to the website.

Article => E-book => Audio => Video's how you can share the same information used in a variety of formats.

Step 13. More, Render:

Here everything is simple. The more you give useful and desirable free, the more you end up with subscribers, customers, and partners.

Look at those who are already very well promoted on the Internet and have a huge subscriber base. You will notice that they give out a huge amount of quality material on a regular basis.

Step 14. Write interesting and often:

Try to bring in their contributions more personality. Find your own style and always use it.

This way you can stand out from the competition,

You start talking about.

If you write a boring or dull copying other people's thoughts, do not rely on the rapid rise.

As for how often to write to the mailing list, then there is a series of completely opposing views.

Someone says that you cannot often make the distribution issues,

Because you can scare all subscribers.

Expert Email-Marketing
Oleg Kolpakov.

I prefer to think that you can write at least 2-3 times a day.

Just write interesting and useful to subscribers.

Do not worry about what people unsubscribe from the mailing list.

Such people tend to never have anything and would not buy.

Always try to model those who really get results from their mailing lists on the Internet. Most interesting is that a large number of subscribers with touches it often leads to an increase in revenues.

Step 15. Mailing Services:

The method that you can implement in just a 5 minutes.

If you're emailing, using any service,

Then you have the ability to easily get about 2 to about 10 subscribers per day.

  To do this, you need to write a letter to support a request to add your e-mail in specific categories in the directory.

Be sure to specify that your mailing complies with all standards of service.

Within a few days, your mail will approve and add to the catalog.

Step 16. Properly position yourself:

You - the expert.

Select a specific narrow niche. Mailing lists "everything about everything" is not read.

Write a few articles and books on specific topics in your niche.

Example. If you are in the niche of personal growth, it is not necessary to write up everything about it.

Select a specific topic, such as neural upgrading or using meditation techniques for personal development.

Expert Email-Marketing
Oleg Kolpakov.

It will be much more attractive. Plus, you'll assist the people this narrow topic.

You will become an expert in it.

I also want to note that the narrower the topic, the more the response from each subscriber.

Step 17. Forums:

2 Find and discussion forums in their bragging rights.

Publish articles; communicate with participants of the forum,

Start dating; organize discussions, polls, etc.

Two forums are enough. Sometimes one is enough.

The forum is an opportunity to make his signature and insert it in the brief description of your site and link to them.

After each left a comment on the forum will be displayed your signature.

You can also negotiate with other participants of the forum post links to your sites in their signatures.

Many are willing to do it for nothing.

Expert Email-Marketing
Oleg Kolpakov.

Step 18. Interviews with experts:

The principle of "Who leads the, from, and rack up" applies in attracting subscribers to the newsletter.

Communicate with those who already have thousands of subscribers in your niche or anything, and try to show all that you do it.

To this end, this option is very suitable for an interview.

If you take an interesting interview already hyped online businessman, you are automatically part of the untwisted and attention to carry on.

Some followers of the interviewee will be transferred to you.

Expert Email-Marketing
Oleg Kolpakov.

Agree, if you record the interview with the president in a cafe in an informal atmosphere, it will cause a lot of interest among the public and start talking about your people...

But an interview with the president does not always work, and it is not always necessary. It is enough to talk and interview with the top-end of all the people in your chosen niche.

In addition, it will bring a good reputation; it also dramatically increases your expert in the eyes of others.

It is a fact. If you are dealing with a tough guy, and that means you too cool :) Interviews can take in a text format, in audio or video.

Expert Email-Marketing
Oleg Kolpakov.

Write some interesting questions, and arrange a specific time of the interview.

It is best to work interview in video format.

Once you have recorded a video, you can also convert audio and text formats for the maximum possible promotion on the Internet.

Take 10-15 interviewing people with many thousand databases of subscribers and you have a solid subscription base will be they.

Pray always, to the one with whom you interviewed,

Also, he made the announcement on its base. It can literally 1day bring you

Expert Email-Marketing
Oleg Kolpakov.

hundreds or even thousands of new subscribers.

Step 19. Ask your subscribers:

Do not be afraid to ask.

If at least a few hundred subscribers you already have a database, then send them in a separate letter, in which he asked them to share your content.

The most interesting thing is that people are quite happy to go to the meeting and help you unwind.

Step 20. Own Affiliate Program:

Affiliate Sales => Money => Advertisement => Subscribers => Partners => private affiliate program - one of a powerful way to attract subscribers.

Using the partner you can attract thousands of new subscribers for a short time and without any cash investment. More precisely, you do not risk your money,

Investing in advertising.

Partners, you pay only for the committed sale.

Now I'll tell you how it happens...

Expert Email-Marketing
Oleg Kolpakov.

Partners receive a referral link that leads you "capture page". In other words, anything partners do not sell, they only recommend your free materials, which can be obtained in exchange for contact information.

And you through your newsletter should already make sales.

If your partner has attracted followers, and the subscriber,

Reading your letter, something you have bought, then the partner gets their deserved commission.

If you have a number of partners with large databases of subscribers very soon, and you organized solid base readers by only a few partnership announcements.

Expert Email-Marketing
Oleg Kolpakov.

Alternatively, you can create a step by step training course for partners, which tell us about the first steps,

You need to do to make your affiliate program. This course can help greatly partner's beginners.

It would be good to prepare more material for partners. This can be articles, letters for mailing,

Banners, statuses for social networks, etc.

The most important thing is to prepare a letter to the announcement in your ezine,

Since it is through distribution partners, most energetically promoting affiliate products.

And one more recommendation, which is why a few people should be.

Expert Email-Marketing
Oleg Kolpakov.

Communicate with your partner every individual,

Negotiate with them on joint promotions, high commission, etc.

Everyone wants an individual approach, so give it to your partner.

 The affiliate program is now on the Internet a huge amount of interest, try it your affiliate program.

Conclusion:

Summing up, I want to note that all of the above ways to

attract subscribers have been tested by me have brought and bring better results every day.

If you also want to get results by increasing the number of your subscribers on a daily basis, you begin to implement the knowledge gained today make sense to delay I do not see tomorrow.

Dear reader, for your interest and reading my book!

I wish you success in business online!

Expert Email-Marketing:

Oleg Kolpakov.

www.ingramcontent.com/pod-product-compliance
Lightning Source LLC
Chambersburg PA
CBHW040919180526
45159CB00002BA/531